A Litany of Saints
Coloring Book
For Kids and Adults

This Book Belongs to:

_____

Mary, Mother of God — Pray for Us.

St. Joseph — Pray for Us.

St. Joan of Arc — Pray for Us.

St. Patrick — Pray for Us.

St. Bernadette — Pray for Us.

St. Padre Pio — Pray for Us.

For my boys.
I will always love you more than the world.

~Mom

Illustrated by Beth Ann Ramos
Published by Good Day Books
First Edition

Learn more at www.bethannramos.com.

good day
BOOKS

Mary, Mother of God

Pray for Us.

St. Blaise

Pray for Us.

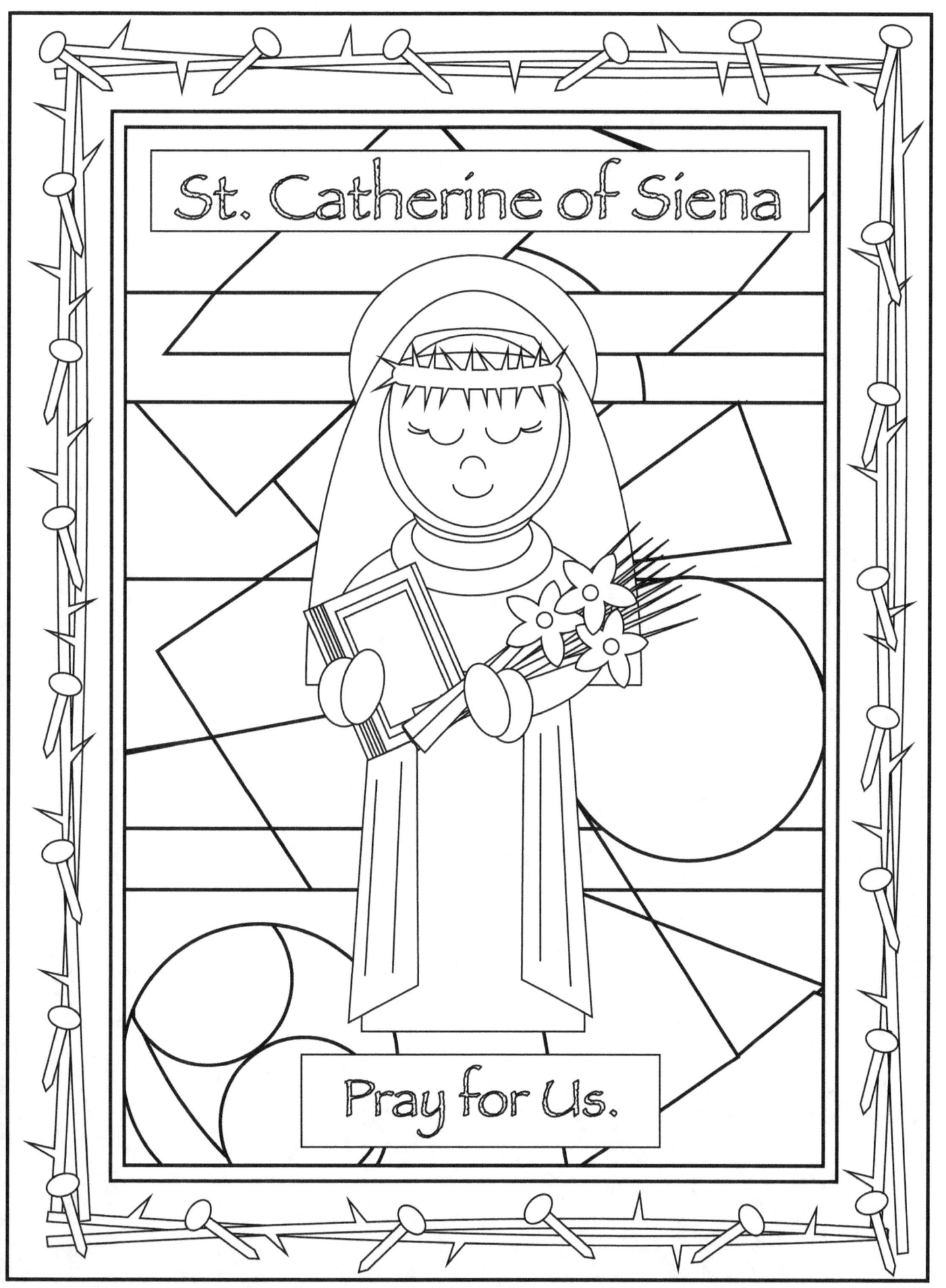

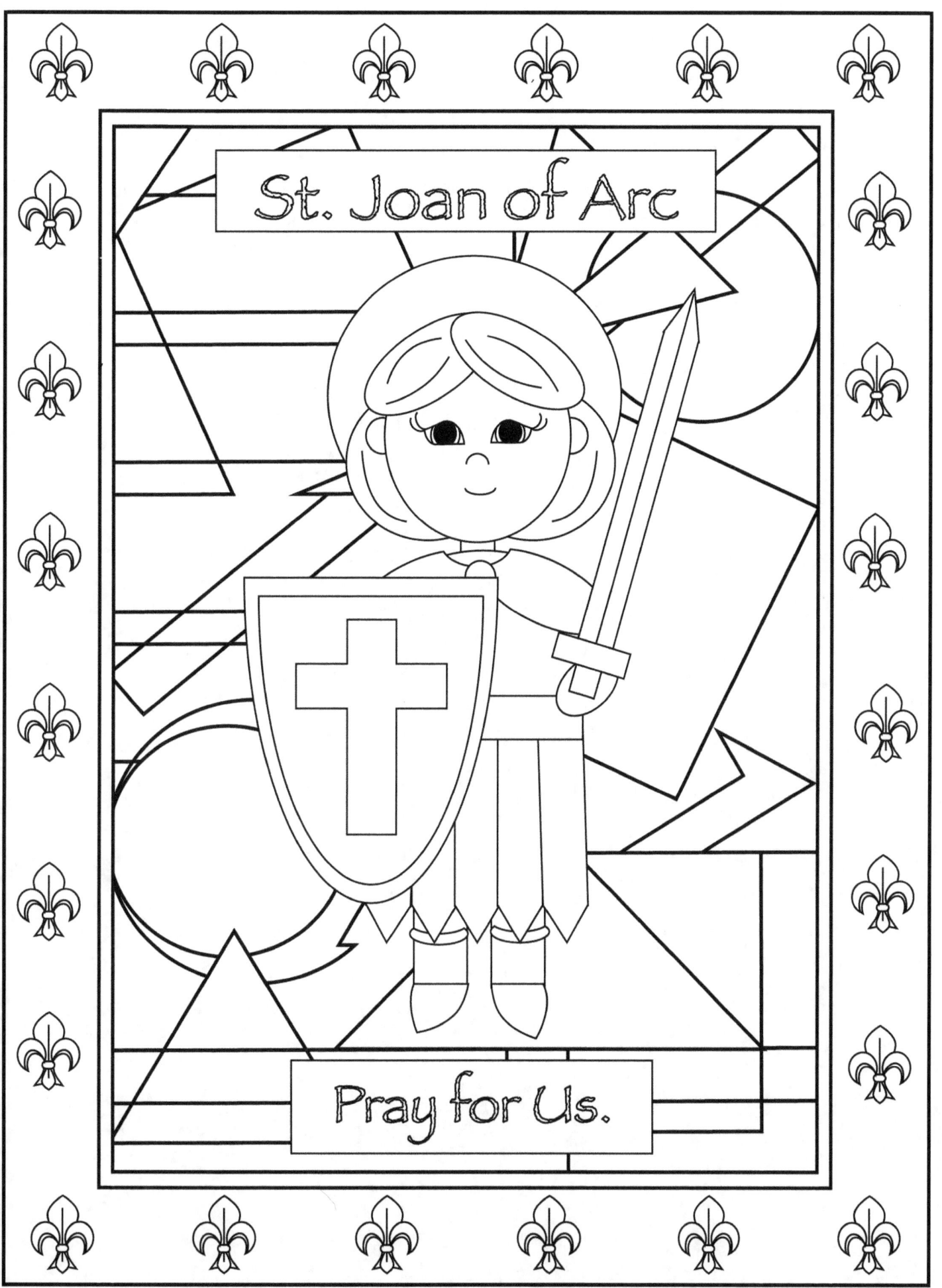

St. Padre Pío

Pray for Us.

Also Available

SAINT SAYINGS
about
The Eucharist
A Picture Book for Catholic Kids

Illustrated by Beth Ann Ramos

SAINT SAYINGS
about
The Eucharist
A Coloring Book for Catholic Kids

Illustrated by Beth Ann Ramos

Free activities and coloring pages available at:
www.bethannramos.com/eucharist

Email books@bethannramos.com
to inquire about bulk or white label pricing for your
school, church, or diocese!